ACTS
LECTIO DIVINA FOR YOUTH

ACTS

LECTIO DIVINA FOR YOUTH

ANCIENT FAITH SERIES

Barefoot Ministries®
Kansas City, Missouri

Copyright 2008 by Barefoot Ministries®

ISBN 978-0-8341-5027-0

Printed in the United States of America

Written by Mark Moore
Editor: Mike Wonch
Assistant Editor: Catherine M. Shaffer
Cover Design: JR Caines
Interior Design: Sharon Page

Adapted from *Lectio Divina Bible Studies: Listening for God Through Acts.*

Moore, Mark. *Lectio Divina Bible Studies: Listening for God Through Acts.* Indianapolis, IN: Wesleyan Publishing House and Beacon Hill Press of Kansas City, 2006.

Library of Congress Control Number: 2008934663

10 9 8 7 6 5 4 3 2 1

ABOUT THE
LECTIO DIVINA
BIBLE STUDIES

Lectio divina (pronounced lek-tsee-oh dih-vee-nuh), is a Latin phrase that means *sacred reading*. It is the ancient Christian practice of communicating with God through the reading and study of Scripture. Throughout history, great Christian leaders have used and adapted this ancient method of interpreting Scripture.

The idea behind *lectio divina* is to look at a Bible passage in such a way that Bible study becomes less about study and more about listening. The approach is designed to focus our attention on what God is saying to us through the Word. Through the process of *lectio divina* we not only read to understand with our minds, but we read to hear with our hearts and obey. It is a way of listening to God through His Word.

Some throughout history have said that *lectio divina* turns Bible study on its head—normally we read the Bible, but in *lectio divina, the Bible reads us*. That is probably a good way to describe it. It is God using His Word in a conversation with us to read into our lives and speak to our hearts.

In this series, we will use the traditional *lectio divina* model. We have expanded each component so that it can be used by both individuals and by groups. Each session in this study includes the following elements. (Latin words and their pronunciation are noted in parentheses.)

- **Reading** (*Lectio* "lek-tsee-oh"). We begin with a time of quieting ourselves prior to reading. Then we take a slow, careful reading of a passage of Scripture. We focus our minds on the central theme of the passage. When helpful, we read out loud or read the same passage over and over several times.
- **Meditation** (*Meditatio* "medi-tah-tsee-oh"). Next, we explore the meaning of the Bible passage. Here we dig deep to try to un-

derstand all of what God might be saying to us. We think on the passage. We explore the images, and pay attention to the emotions and feelings that the passage provides. We put ourselves in the story. We look for particular words or phrases that leap off the page as the Spirit begins to speak to us through the Word.

- **Prayer** (*Oratio* "or-ah-tsee-oh"). As we meditate on the passage, we respond to God by communicating with Him. We specifically ask God to speak to us through His Word. We begin to dialog with Him about what we have read. We express praise, thanksgiving, confession, or agreement to God. And we listen. We wait before Him in silence, allowing God the chance to speak.

- **Contemplation** (*Contemplatio* "con-tehm-plah-tsee-oh"). At this point in our conversation through the Word, we come to a place where we rest in the presence of God. Our study is now about receiving what He has said to us. Imagine two old friends who have just talked at length—and now without words, they just sit together and enjoy each other's presence. Having spent time listening to God, we know a little better how God is shaping the direction of our lives. Here there is a yielding of oneself to God's will. We resolve to act on the message of Scripture.

GROUP STUDY

This book is designed to be useful for both individual and group study. To use this in a group, you may take one of several approaches:

- **Individual Study/Group Review**. Make sure each member of the group has a copy of the book. Have them read through one section during the week. (They will work through the same passage or portions of it each day that week.) Then, when you meet together, review what thoughts, notes, and insights the members of the group experienced in their individual study. Use the group questions at the end of the section as a guide.

- **Group Lectio**. Make sure each member of the group has a copy of the book. Have them read through one section during the week in individual study. When you meet together as a group, you will study the passage together through a reading form similar to lectio divina:

- ○ **First, read the passage out loud several times to the group.** Group members respond by waiting in silence and letting God speak.
- ○ **Second, have the passage read aloud again to the group once or twice more.** Use different group members for different voices, and have them read slowly. Group members listen for a word or two that speaks to them, and share it with the group. Break into smaller groups if appropriate.
- ○ **Third, read the passage out loud again, and have the group pray together to ask God what He might be saying to each person, and to the group as a whole.** Go around and share what each person is learning from this process. At this point, review together the group questions at the end of the section.[1]

- • **Lectio Divina Steps for Groups.** Make sure each member has a copy of the book. As a group, move through the study together, going through each of the parts: reading, meditation, prayer, and contemplation. Be sure to use the group questions at the end of the section.

The important thing about using *lectio divina* in a group is to remember that this is to be incarnational ("in the flesh")—in other words, we begin to live out the Word in our community. We carry God's Word in us, (in the flesh, or incarnate in us) and we carry that Word into our group to be lived out among them.

The *Lectio Divina Bible Studies* invite readers to slow down, read Scripture, meditate upon it, and prayerfully respond to God's Word.

---

1. Parts of the "Group Lectio" section adapted from Tony Jones, *The Sacred Way: Spiritual Practices for Everyday Life*, Grand Rapids: Zondervan, 2005, p. 54.

CONTENTS

INTRODUCTION

Acts reads as a sequel to the Gospel of Luke. Most likely written by the same author, Acts is equally systematic, well-researched, and clearly written. It reports the birth, infancy, and explosive growth of the Church of Jesus Christ, picking up the story at the day of Jesus' ascension and continuing to about A.D. 63.

Acts centers on the same character as Luke's Gospel, Jesus of Nazareth. In this second book, however, Jesus only speaks twice—in chapter 1, witnessed by a crowd of people; and again in chapter 9, seen and heard clearly by only one man. Still, Jesus' presence fills the book from beginning to end.

As in any good sequel, the supporting characters in Acts grow and mature, and new characters are added as the story unfolds. One of the most important characters is the Holy Spirit, who enters energetically in chapter 2.

The remarkable action in Acts is every bit as heart-pounding as in the Gospel: the conversion of 3,000 people in one day, the stoning of Stephen, the imprisonment of faithful followers, the transformation of malicious Saul into fearless Paul. The Book of Acts is a spectacular dramatization of the time after Jesus' ascension. Through the power of the Holy Spirit, the disciples were enabled to spread the gospel and establish the Church. "And the Lord added to their number daily those who were being saved" (Acts 2:47*b*).

THE ASCENDING
SAVIOR

LISTENING FOR GOD THROUGH ACTS 1:1-14

SUMMARY

The stunned disciples peered up into the thickening clouds, speechless, until they were startled by the presence of angels. Jesus had risen from the dead. He was really there, walking with them, discussing the kingdom of God with them, breaking bread with them; then in a moment, He was gone.

The men dressed in white reassured the disciples that Jesus would return again, but this was not what they expected the Messiah to do. He had already returned from the grave, and now He was supposed to save Israel and establish His mighty kingdom.

Jesus did begin building God's kingdom that day; He just didn't do it in the way anyone on earth expected. His simple promise of the Holy Spirit foreshadowed the coming power that would enable the disciples—ordinary fisherman—to lead a revolution that has changed the world.

As you meditate on this passage, put yourself in the disciples' shoes, experiencing the myriad of emotions they must have felt as their Savior ascended.

PREPARATION ✚ FOCUS YOUR THOUGHTS

Have you ever had a close friend or family member move away? Have you ever watched the plane carrying the person you love disappear into a fog of clouds?

Experience those feelings again.

READING ✚ HEAR THE WORD

Although we don't know for certain who wrote the Book of Acts, a few clues lean largely in the direction of Luke, the physician and Gospel writer. Theophilus, the recipient of this book, was also the recipient of the Gospel of Luke, where he was addressed as "most excellent," possibly referring to a high governmental position. The author addressing Theophilus in the introduction claims to have written a previous book chronicling the life of Jesus. Luke was one of a few of Paul's close travel companions and proves to be the most logical author of Acts.

The disciples were surprised by Jesus' ascension in this passage because Jewish tradition held that the Anointed One would come and restore the nation of Israel to a place of prominence and power as God's chosen people. This wasn't the first plot twist Jesus offered in the story of the Messiah. His suffering and death were not humanly expected parts of the restoration process, especially His execution as a criminal.

The Ascension, however, like the Crucifixion, was a vital part in God's plan for restoration. In the Gospel of John, Jesus encouraged His disciples, telling them that though He must go back to the One who sent Him, He was sending another, a Comforter, who would flood them with grace and power. The promised gift from the Father exploded onto the scene shortly after Jesus left, and the Church ignited.

Read Acts 1:1-14 slowly with a spirit of prayer, asking God to open your eyes to the meaning of the text.

MEDITATION ✝ ENGAGE THE WORD

Meditate on Acts 1:1-5

The writer of the Book of Acts addressed his familiar friend, Theophilus, with a reminder of his last writings which covered "all that Jesus began to do and to teach" (1:1). Imagine being a news reporter for your school paper and your assignment is to chronicle the life of the most famous man who ever lived: Jesus of Nazareth. What would you write about? What stories would you highlight?

Recall the Gospel accounts of the life and ministry of Jesus.

What was the main point of Jesus' life? What was the heart of His message?

In verse 5, Jesus contrasts the water baptism of John with the coming baptism of the Holy Spirit by fire. What is the difference between these two baptisms?

Meditate on Acts 1:6-8

The disciples were constantly missing the point. They made assumptions about how God was going to act, how Israel would be restored. Can you think of an area in your life in which you may be missing the point with God? Do you have a certain way you think He should act? How do you react when He doesn't meet your expectations?

Jesus didn't answer the disciples' questions with specifics. He did make them a promise: they would receive the Holy Spirit and be witnesses of His love to the entire world. What are some promises God has made to you that haven't necessarily answered your questions but have moved you beyond them? What are some things you expect from God based on your own perceptions and what are some things about God can you be sure of?

Read the quote from David Kirk on page 17. What does he mean by the "final kingdom of shalom"? List a few of the many ways we are to be signs of the kingdom of God.

We are living "between the times"—the time of Christ's resurrection and the new age of the Spirit, and the time of fulfillment in Christ. Life in the Spirit is a pledge, a "down-payment," on the final kingdom of shalom. In the meantime, we are to be signs of the kingdom which is, and which is coming. —David Kirk

Meditate on Acts 1:9-11

The scene of Jesus disappearing seems to come right out of Hollywood. What is the significance of His ascension through the clouds?

The angels reassured the awestruck disciples that Jesus would return in a similar manner. What do you think that means? Is He literally going to come back riding the clouds? How do you picture His second coming happening?

Read the quote from William Temple. How do you understand the accessibility of Jesus after His ascension compared to the days of His ministry?

In the days of His earthly ministry, only those could speak to him who came where He was: if He was in Galilee, men could not find Him in Jerusalem; if He was in Jerusalem, men could not find Him in Galilee. His Ascension means that He is perfectly united with God; we are with Him wherever we are present to God; and that is everywhere and always. —William Temple

Meditate on Acts 1:12-14

Examine closely the scenario of the disciples and the women joining together in incessant prayer. What characteristics of true Christian community can you draw from this picture?

Considering His mother's and brothers' previous confusion concerning Jesus' ministry, how do you think their perception of Jesus changed after being witnesses to His death, resurrection, and ascension?

As you meditate on this passage, envision sitting in the Upper Room with this group. Feel the tension of sorrow and joy, the confusion of a missing Messiah, the excitement of what's to come.

PRAYER ✝ ASK AND LISTEN

Seek the face of God. Ask, "Lord, what are You saying to us today?"

After the awesome experience of Jesus ascending into heaven, the disciples, along with the women followers, gathered in an upper room and *prayed constantly.* What would it look like for you to pray constantly?

Ask God to give you a spirit of continuous prayer.

CONTEMPLATION ✝ REFLECT AND YIELD

Do you find it hard to follow God when you are confused by His actions? Does God always meet your expectations?

Read the quote from Anatole France. In His sovereignty, God often works without being noticed or praised. What circumstances in your life, which you previously attributed to *chance*, may have been the anonymous workings of God?

> *Chance is perhaps the pseudonym of God when he does not wish to sign his work.* —Anatole France

GROUP STUDY

- Why do you think the disciples were surprised by Jesus' ascension? How do you think you would have reacted if you had been in their place?

- Do you think the disciples' faith faltered when they realized Jesus was once again leaving them? If so, why?

- Have you ever felt like God has deserted you? What do you do to fight these feelings?

- What are the ways we can feel God's presence in our lives?

- Try journaling the top stories of God's amazing work and love in your life. Record times of rescue, forgiveness, and faithfulness. Share these events with a friend from your group.

THE SPARK THAT IGNITED A CHURCH

LISTENING FOR GOD THROUGH ACTS 2:32-47

SUMMARY

The Messiah had come. Jesus' ministry had fulfilled the promises of the prophets of old, and now His promise of the arrival of a great Comforter was fulfilled as Peter addressed the crowd and sparked a flame that ignited a worldwide movement of followers of Christ—the Church.

The truth of God's Word sliced open the hearts of His chosen people. God himself had paid the debt for the sin of His children. Peter's call to repentance and cleansing was received by 3,000 contrite hearts that Day of Pentecost.

The presence of the Holy Spirit unified this large group nearly instantaneously, establishing the Church as one body with many parts dedicated to the service of one mission. The Early Church remains for us a lasting example of sacrificial love and selfless devotion.

PREPARATION ✠ FOCUS YOUR THOUGHTS

Have you ever been a witness to the beginning of life? Imagine experiencing the same sense of creation as an early Christian at the birth of the universal Church.

READING ✠ HEAR THE WORD

In the 14th chapter of John's Gospel, Jesus comforted His disciples as He explained to them the motive behind His coming, suffering, and death. As He broke bread with them in the Upper Room, Jesus made a promise that the Father would send a helper, a *parakleôtos.* Jesus insisted that He had to leave them in order for the Spirit to come. Jesus wasn't the only one who foretold the outpouring of the Holy Spirit. God made this promise to His people through the prophets, a fact Peter referred to by quoting the prophet Joel in his Pentecost passage.

Peter also used the Book of Psalms in his explanation of the kingship of Jesus. The quote from David comes from Psalm 110 and is an example of prophetic poetry looking ahead at the relationship between Jesus and His Father. Peter pointed out that David was not speaking of himself in this psalm, a point that opened the eyes of many listening to him.

In the portion of Psalm 110 not referenced by Peter, David went on to call this "lord" [Jesus] a priest in the order of

Melchizedek, directing his Jewish audience back to Abraham and ultimately the initial promise of salvation.

Read Acts 2:32-47 aloud twice, paying special attention to verses 42-47.

MEDITATION ✝ ENGAGE THE WORD

Meditate on Acts 2:32-36

These four simple verses address one of the most complex concepts in all of Scripture: the inner working of the Trinity. The Father raised the Son to His right hand. The Holy Spirit was promised and sent by both the Father and the Son. They are all three distinct persons yet one God and Lord.

Peter quoted David in his Pentecost sermon. What was David's understanding of the Messiah? Do you think Jesus would have fit David's messianic mold? Read Psalm 110 as you meditate on this question.

Read the quote from John Wesley on page 24. What do you think Wesley meant when he spoke of setting up the kingdom of heaven on earth? You don't have to be a pastor to be one of Wesley's hundred. Understanding this, is there anything stopping you from joining this group?

> Give me one hundred preachers who fear nothing but
> sin and desire nothing but God, and I care not whether
> they be clergymen or laymen, they alone will shake the
> gates of Hell and set up the kingdom of Heaven upon
> Earth.   —John Wesley

Meditate on Acts 2:37-41

Do you remember a time when God pierced your false defenses and opened your heart to His life? Have you ever seen this happen in someone else's life? What is the true cause of this brokenness?

Read the quote from A. W. Tozer. Peter's call for repentance and baptism came with a gift, the Holy Spirit. Have you ever thought that being Spirit-filled was only something for super-Christians? What does it mean to be full of the Spirit?

> The Spirit-filled life is not a special, deluxe edition of
> Christianity. It is part and parcel of the total plan of
> God for his people.   —A. W. Tozer

The outpouring of the Holy Spirit occurred after Jesus' resurrection and ascension and after the disciples believed Jesus as the Christ. Is there a time lapse between the moment of belief and the gift of the Holy Spirit for Christians today?

Read the quote from Charles Spurgeon. Peter definitely served it up hot. Has the fire of your baptism seemed more like a waning flame lately?

> Religion is a dish to be served hot; once it becomes lukewarm it is sickening. Our baptism must be with the Holy Ghost and with fire if we would win the masses to hear the gospel. —Charles Spurgeon

Meditate on Acts 2:42-47

This is the premier passage of biblical community. How might these verses have an impact on the Church today?

The believers sold their possessions and held everything in common in an act that many call *Christian socialism.* What were the benefits of this economic venture? Is it possible to accomplish this in today's market? Should we attempt to move back to this sort of communal economy? Why, or why not?

Read the quote from Philip Yancey on page 26. Now that Jesus is in heaven and the Spirit has come, what is the Church supposed to do? In what ways can we model the kingdom of heaven on earth?

> *The people of God are not merely to mark time, wait-*
> *ing for God to step in and set right all that is wrong.*
> *Rather, they are to model the new heaven and new*
> *earth, and by so doing awaken longing for what God*
> *will someday bring to pass.* —Philip Yancey

Look past the socioeconomic message of this description of the Early Church. What does it say about the correct spirit of the Church? Does anything in your church need to change for true fellowship to occur? How can you be part of that change?

PRAYER ✠ ASK AND LISTEN

Seek the face of God. Ask, "Lord, what are You saying to us today?"

Throughout Acts we see believers praying together fervently before the Lord. Pray together that God will pour out His Spirit on your group, your church, and your community.

CONTEMPLATION ✠ REFLECT AND YIELD

Verses 42-47 show the *agape* love of early believers. Do you think the same type of unity is occurring among Christians today? Why, or why not?

What is the current Church devoted to?

GROUP STUDY

- How do you understand the Trinity (Father, Son, and Holy Spirit)? What does this passage say about the different roles of each member of this holy threesome?

- Have you experienced the presence of the Holy Spirit in your life? How does this presence affect the way you live?

- How does your church compare to the Acts 2 church? What can you do to make your church more like the biblical model?

- We are told that God will spit those out of His mouth who are lukewarm in their faith (Rev. 3:15-16). What are some ways to keep your relationship with God aflame?

- Sharing a meal together is a critical part of fellowship. Families strengthen around the dinner table and friends grow closer when they eat together. Plan a meal with either family or friends this week.

THE WISDOM OF A PHARISEE
LISTENING FOR GOD THROUGH ACTS 5:27-42

SUMMARY

Founded on the belief that salvation is rendered by the death and resurrection of Jesus Christ, the movement known as the Way began to spread. Fearful Jewish leaders sought to squelch any momentum of this rising faction by having its main members brought before their high court. Peter and the other apostles stood on trial for preaching the name of Jesus. These Jewish officials were enraged that they were being blamed for executing the Messiah to the point that they wanted to put to death anyone who spoke His name.

One of their own, though, brought a word of wisdom to their counsel. He advised his brothers to let God work things out. If God was truly behind this movement, then not even the death of its leaders would stop it. God would work His will regardless of the players involved, and they did not want to be on the side that warred against God. The council listened to him, and the apostles—after being scorned and beaten— were released.

Upon being released, the apostles proclaimed the good news of the salvation of Jesus Christ with even more zeal.

PREPARATION ⳾ Focus Your Thoughts

Have you ever been faced with a major life decision? Was it a time when the will of God wasn't exactly clear? How did you seek out the will of the Father?

READING ⳾ Hear the Word

Peter and the other apostles were taken before the Sanhedrin, the highest Jewish court. This court worked primarily like our Supreme Court works today. It saw cases the lower courts could not decide on, and it interpreted and enforced the main law of the people—for them, the Law of Moses. The Sanhedrin consisted of 71 members and 2 major schools of thought, the Pharisees and the Sadducees. The deciding difference of these two parties was the belief in the resurrection of the dead, which the Pharisees held to be true and the Sadducees did not.

Gamaliel was a Pharisee, a wise and respected man. He was one of the apostle Paul's main teachers. Gamaliel's wisdom and sensitivity to the will of God may have been the first seed of openness to Jesus' resurrection planted deep within Paul's heart.

Read Acts 5:27-42 and visualize yourself sitting among the council, listening to the testimony of the apostles and Gamaliel's warning.

MEDITATION ☧ ENGAGE THE WORD

Meditate on Acts 5:27-28

Standing before the highest court in the land, Peter and the other apostles were forbidden to speak the name of Jesus. How is the ruling of the Sanhedrin similar with recent rulings given by the Supreme Court in the United States? In what ways are we restricted from speaking the name of Jesus?

Read the quote from G. K. Chesterton. We see glimpses of it today, but a time may be coming when even speaking the name of Jesus will require great courage. In what countries right now is it a crime to speak openly about Christianity? Would you have the courage to speak His name?

> Brave men are all vertebrates; they have their softness on the surface and their toughness in the middle.
>
> —G. K. Chesterton

Meditate on Acts 5:29-32

Peter's passionate response raises for us an interesting question: when is it permissible to go against a direct order of the state? How do we balance the principle of respecting those in authority over us against following the truth of God?

Using verses 30-32, define the gospel, the good news of Jesus Christ.

Read the quote from Daniel Webster. Do you struggle with accepting the fantastic gospel story as a reality? Could this story of Jesus be just that: a simple, moral story? To have any meaning, is it necessary for the events explained by Peter to the Sanhedrin to be factual? Do you think the disciples would have risked their lives for a myth? Would you give up your life for a story?

> My heart has always assured and reassured me that the gospel of Christ must be a Divine reality.
>
> —Daniel Webster

Meditate on Acts 5:33-39

Gamaliel's address to the members of the council was poignant and wise, yet it came from a seemingly unlikely source. Has God ever spoken His wisdom to you through an unusual source? Considering God as the source of all truth, what are some other places one can find His truth outside the general Christian community?

Gamaliel associated the Way with other revolts that had occurred in the area. Is Christianity truly a revolt against Judaism? Explain the connection between the old covenant and the new covenant. How did Jesus view these two testaments?

Read the quote from C. S. Lewis. How are you affected by your circle of friends? Is your current group of friends making you wiser or dumbing you down? What are some things you can do to help improve your own wisdom?

> The next best thing to being wise oneself is to live in a circle of those who are. —C. S. Lewis

Meditate on Acts 5:40-42

Though the apostles were set free, they still had to endure a flogging. What is the price of freedom today? Have you ever suffered for doing what is right? Would you humbly rejoice in being counted worthy to suffer disgrace for the sake of Christ?

The disciples would not—could not!—stop preaching the name of Jesus. Do you feel this strong drive to share His Word? How can you proclaim His name in your community?

PRAYER ✟ ASK AND LISTEN

Seek the face of God. Ask, "Lord, what are You saying to us today?"

Understanding the will of God can take a bit of trial and error. Are you currently involved in something that causes you to question whether your motive is humanly-inspired or God-driven? Pray for discernment. Pray for wisdom and understanding.

CONTEMPLATION ✟ REFLECT AND YIELD

How do you know whether something is of human origin or from God? What tests can you use to help find the truth?

Read the quote from B. A. Copass. Do you find it hard to take Jesus at His word? Why do you think so much of God's truth seems like a mystery?

> *God has revealed many truths which He has not ex-*
> *plained. We will just have to be content to let Him*
> *know some things we do not and take Him at His*
> *word.* —B. A. Copass

GROUP STUDY

- What does it mean to have religious freedom?

- Do you take advantage of your freedom to share your faith with others?

- Daniel Webster said that his heart reassured him of God's existence. Do you have a *head* belief or a *heart* belief in God? Is one more important than the other?

- God used Gamaliel to protect the apostles. Do you think God commonly uses non-Christians to accomplish His will? If so, how?

- Share your dreams with God and ask Him to lead you to His will. Then ask Him for the courage required to follow your calling.

THE STONING OF STEPHEN

LISTENING FOR GOD THROUGH ACTS 7:39-60

SUMMARY

As the movement of the Way continued to grow, the apostles found it necessary to appoint lay workers (deacons) to oversee the work of distributing food to orphans and widows, among other service tasks. Stephen was chosen as one of seven to do this job, but as Stephen began his work and shared his faith, God called him to a higher act of service.

Stephen unabashedly preached the good news of Jesus Christ and never lowered his voice in fear, even when standing before the mighty Sanhedrin. Stephen was a common disciple, but his words that day were anything but common. They were extraordinary. They were full of passion and confidence founded on the grace and love of his Savior.

As the stones began to hit and cloaks were strewn at the feet of Saul in praise of his zealous killings, Stephen received his glorious reward as a martyr. His death had the opposite effect from what the Sanhedrin had hoped. Instead of fear, courage spread among the believers. Instead of silence, a growing war cry could be heard.

PREPARATION ✞ FOCUS YOUR THOUGHTS

Have you ever had to exert your energy to the point of physical exhaustion? Maybe it was on the athletic field, at school, or the simple daily drain of going without sleep.

We can't fully understand the plight of the martyr (one who dies for his or her faith) but we can at least grasp the feeling of utter exhaustion.

READING ✞ HEAR THE WORD

The newly formed body of Christ grew at such a rapid pace that the 12 disciples could not do everything that needed to be done. They couldn't do all the preaching and teaching and ministry of the Word while they were caring for the physical needs of the people. The seven who were chosen by the disciples, recorded in Acts 6, were men full of the Holy Spirit and wisdom. They would be considered deacons in the current church, a word that comes from the Greek word *diakoneo*, which literally means "table waiter."

This didn't mean the disciples no longer had to serve people, but the majority of their time was reserved for prayer and teaching. The deacons looked after the daily affairs of the pooled resources of the early believers much like a manager would do.

As Peter did in his speech on the Day of Pentecost, Stephen passionately tried to persuade the Jewish Sanhedrin by appealing to the words of their prophets who spoke of Jesus' coming, quoting passages from Amos and Isaiah. These passages prophesied, though, to the fact that the children of Israel would harden their hearts against the message of Christ.

Read Acts 7:39-60. Read this long passage slowly, and put yourself in the place of the Jewish leaders. Is your heart hardened to the will of God?

MEDITATION ☦ ENGAGE THE WORD

Meditate on Acts 7:39-43

The children of Israel were constantly turning their backs on God and running into the arms of idols. What idols in your life keep you from running to the true God? Do you find yourself in an endless cycle of putting your trust in idols rather than God?

Stephen's speech before the Sanhedrin was one of many attempts by the early Christians to share the message of Christ with the highest Jewish officials. Why were their hearts so hardened to the message of Jesus?

Read the quote from Martin Luther. Why are we so easily attracted to idolatry? Are there subtle ways that we exalt simple things of nature over God?

> We easily fall into idolatry, for we are inclined thereunto by nature, and coming to us by inheritance, it seems pleasant.   —Martin Luther

Meditate on Acts 7:44-50

In his appeal, Stephen referred to the "tabernacle of testimony," which would have symbolized for the Jewish leaders the very presence of God. Where does God's presence reside now? How can people be so close to God and still miss Him? In what ways have you been blinded to His presence?

Does God feel distant to you? He is closer than you feel Him to be. Ask Him to open your heart to recognize His presence.

Meditate on Acts 7:51-53

The chosen people of God were in many ways the worst at perceiving His work and accepting it with joy. How were they resisting the Holy Spirit? How do we resist the Holy Spirit?

The Israelites were not the only nation known for killing messengers of tough truth. What would cause an entire nation to reject the message of just one of its citizens?

Read the quote from John Calvin. What are some typical causes of unbelief? Has unbelief caused you to miss any of God's blessings? How do you deal with doubt and unbelief?

> *No man is excluded from calling upon God, the gate of salvation is set open unto all men: neither is there any other thing which keepeth us back from entering in, save only our own unbelief.* —John Calvin

Stephen spoke of the Law being "put into effect through angels." I don't think that this is a huge theological issue, but what do you think he meant by that statement? Is there any great significance that angels had a hand in instituting God's law?

Meditate on Acts 7:54-60

In a moment of the leaders' fury, Stephen entered God's glorious presence a martyr. Have you heard any contemporary stories of martyrdom? Share some of these stories as a group and marvel at the courage and zeal of God's saints.

Read the quote from church father Augustine on page 42. News about suicide bombers and terrorists fulfilling their callings as martyrs for their faith fills the airwaves these days. What makes Stephen's death different from other types of martyrs? For what sort of causes can someone truly be considered a martyr?

> *Not the punishment but the cause makes the martyr.*
> —*Augustine*

Stephen carried the spirit of Christ with him until the very end, even breathing out forgiveness for his killers as he died. How was Stephen able to remain so full of love during this traumatic event? Would his reaction have been your natural instinct?

Read the quote from Søren Kierkegaard. Why doesn't the death of a martyr kill his cause? How did the movement of Jesus Christ enlarge after Stephen's death?

> *The tyrant dies and his rule is over, the martyr dies and his rule begins.* — *Søren Kierkegaard*

While actual martyrdom in North America is low, across the world hundreds of thousands of people are being imprisoned and dying each year for their faith. Yet despite overt persecution, the international church is exploding. What can the North American church learn from our international brothers and sisters?

PRAYER ✠ ASK AND LISTEN

Seek the face of God. Ask, "Lord, what are You saying to us today?"

Stephen saw beyond this world as he looked up into the face of Jesus. He had no fear, because he saw his Comforter. He saw his Savior and the place He had prepared for him.

Pray with the same sense of comfort. Look up into heaven and seek God's face.

CONTEMPLATION ✠ REFLECT AND YIELD

How did Stephen and the many martyrs who followed him affect the course of the Early Church? How was this persecution helpful in spreading the gospel?

Honestly wrestle with this question: Would you be willing to endure persecution, even death, for the cause of Christ?

GROUP STUDY

- Have you encountered someone who was hostile toward the Christian story? How did you respond to that person?

- Have you encountered persecution because of your faith? If so, how and why?

- What have been some positive outcomes as a result of standing firm in your faith?

- Stephen's martyrdom sparked a renewed courage in Christians. What would happen if more Christians today stood up for their faith?

- Think about how God's presence is evident in the Church today. What strength do you gain knowing that God is still at work in the Church right now?

- As a group, locate current stories of persecution. (Check out the book *Foxe: Voices of the Martyrs*.) Discover ways you can help these organizations. Begin by praying each morning for the persecuted.

THE CONVERSION OF PAUL

LISTENING FOR GOD THROUGH ACTS 9:1-16

SUMMARY

The most vicious, violent opponent of the Way was chosen by God to carry Jesus' name to the Gentiles. Surprised? The early Christians couldn't believe it either. Ananias feared Saul, even when sent directly by God. Why? Ananias had heard about this persecutor of Christians and feared for his life. Why would God work in this manner?

From the beginning, God's message has been about total life-transformation. He is not so concerned with making our lives better as with making our lives completely different. Saul's zeal, originally for imprisoning and killing those who believed in the good news of salvation through Jesus Christ, was sanctified and turned into passion for spreading the gospel all over the world.

If God can change the heart of the "chief of sinners," how much more can He change your heart? Your story, like Paul's, will be one of complete change—beautiful reconciliation with the God and Father of all.

PREPARATION ✟ FOCUS YOUR THOUGHTS

Have you ever been driving west around the time the sun was setting and been blinded by its bright light for a brief moment? Imagine that blindness lasting for a couple of days, a couple months, a lifetime. How do you think you would feel if you suddenly went blind?

READING ✟ HEAR THE WORD

In his letter to the Philippians, we learn a little about Paul's Jewish heritage. He was what he called a "Hebrew of Hebrews"—following the letter of the Law. He was from the tribe of Benjamin and a Pharisee. His schooling as a Pharisee, under the wise Gamaliel, actually prepared the way for him to understand the resurrection of Jesus and know how to share it with other Jews.

Damascus was one of the oldest of the ancient cities, mentioned as far back as the time of Abraham. It was the capital of Syria, located about 133 miles north of Jerusalem. Saul's traveling this great distance from Jerusalem showed the immense hatred he had for followers of Jesus.

Straight Street, which was the address where the blind Saul

was staying, was the main street of the city, also referred to as Queens Street.

Ananias was yet another wise, godly man whom God placed in the life of Paul to instruct him and guide him to the truth.

Read Acts 9:1-16 twice, alternating readers every eight verses.

MEDITATION ✠ ENGAGE THE WORD

Meditate on Acts 9:1-6

What is the significance of the flashing light at Saul's conversion? the road? his mission in Damascus?

Jesus spoke directly to Saul at the moment of his salvation. He accused Saul of persecuting Him. Why do you think Jesus personally appeared to Saul on the road to Damascus?

Read the quote from Joseph Alleine. How did the deep work of conversion continue to mature in Paul's life? Explain how conversion is as much a process as it is instantaneous.

> *Conversion is a deep work—a heart-work. It goes throughout the man, throughout the mind, throughout the members, throughout the entire life.*
>
> —Joseph Alleine

Meditate on Acts 9:7-9

Paul was blinded by the light and truth of Christ. While this event truly happened, it also serves as a metaphor of redemption. What does the metaphor of Paul's blindness teach us? What do you think were the reactions of the men traveling with Paul? (Remember: they saw the light but didn't hear the voice.)

Read the quote from John Milton. Think of his poetic words as referring to spiritual blindness. What causes spiritual blindness? In what ways can this sort of blindness be self-inflicted?

> *O loss of sight, of thee I most complain! Blind among enemies, O worse than chains, dungeon or beggary, or decrepit age! Light, the prime work of God, to me is extinct, and all her various objects of delight annulled, which might in part my grief have eased.*
>
> —John Milton

Light is a common symbol of God. What insight does the contrast of dark to light give in the area of conversion?

Read the quote from Thomas Hardy on page 49. Here, Hardy is speaking of a different kind of blindness—illusion. In your eagerness to serve Christ, have you chased after illusions? How can you open your eyes to the true work of God? Saul thought he was following God. He even thought God was pleased with what he was doing by persecuting this heretical sect. But he was chasing an illusion. What illusions are present in the Church today?

> There is a condition worse than blindness, and that is, seeing something that isn't there.   —Thomas Hardy

Meditate on Acts 9:10-16

Ananias probably couldn't have been taken more off guard by God's command to go to Saul, a ruthless enemy. Have you ever been taken off guard by one of Christ's commands? Do you have enemies to whom you are called to minister?

God explained to Ananias that He had chosen Saul as His messenger to the Gentiles. This must have seemed an odd choice to Ananias. Have you ever questioned God about one of His chosen servants? What is God trying to teach us by choosing imperfect people to carry out His perfect will?

Read the quote from Blaise Pascal on page 50. Conversion is not a matter of intention. Intention is rendered powerless without action. Have you put all of your good intentions into action? What is stopping you from being truly changed?

Men often take their imagination for their heart; and they believe they are converted as soon as they think of being converted. —*Blaise Pascal*

PRAYER ✛ ASK AND LISTEN

Seek the face of God. Ask, "Lord, what are You saying to us today?"

Examine your life before the Lord and ask Him to reveal to you how you have been working against Him. Open your heart fully to God in prayer and allow His Spirit to purify you.

CONTEMPLATION ✛ REFLECT AND YIELD

The blindness Saul experienced was both physical and spiritual. While you may not be physically blind, how is your spiritual eyesight? Are your eyes opened wide to what the Lord is doing? Or are they blinded by your own will and desires?

GROUP STUDY

- Why do you think Saul was so strongly opposed to the followers of Christ?

- How was Saul persecuting Jesus? How is Jesus being persecuted today?

- Do you ever feel unworthy of being called one of Christ's servants because of past sins? What can you do to overcome these feelings?

- After Saul was converted, his life changed dramatically. How have you changed since you became a Christian? How do you continue to change?

- Saul's conversion was authentic, but Ananias couldn't have known that. How do you react when God asks you to do something you don't understand? What *should* your reaction be?

- Just as God spoke to Ananias concerning Saul's need, ask Him to show you a person in your life who is walking around spiritually blind. Make an effort to spend some time this week with the person God reveals.

PETER'S VISION CHANGES
LISTENING FOR GOD THROUGH ACTS 10:9-23

SUMMARY

The entire scope of Jewish culture was detailed and directed by the Law of Moses, from the Ten Commandments to strict dietary rules. What the children of Israel ate was just as much a spiritual issue as adultery or murder. Peter's vision was a huge paradigm shift for the Jewish disciples and early followers of Christ. While Jesus was the Messiah—God's Anointed One to save the Jews—His salvation was not meant for just the nation of Israel.

God revealed this to Peter by showing him a change in the Law. What was once considered unclean was suddenly considered clean. God immediately sent men from Cornelius the centurion to get Peter and hear his message. Gentiles were being let in on the great secret of God that Jews had kept since the time of Abraham.

Peter naturally resisted, wanting to show God his holiness; but God had changed the rules of the game. What Peter ate was no longer a sign of his devotion to God. The motivation of his heart was what mattered now.

PREPARATION ☩ FOCUS YOUR THOUGHTS

Have you had a traditional Passover—or any kosher—meal? Why do you think God gave such strict food preparation guidelines to the children of Israel? Discuss a few of the dietary laws and God's possible motives.

READING ☩ HEAR THE WORD

In this passage of Acts we find Peter praying on a rooftop, a custom he learned from the Savior. A typical Jewish house at this time would normally have a rooftop that served as another room. Peter became hungry and was awaiting a kosher meal when he received this vision. The dietary laws found in the Book of Leviticus shed light on this vision.

The 11th chapter of Leviticus details what kind of food would be considered kosher. The Jews were allowed to eat only of animals that had split hooves and chewed cud; so when Peter saw a sheet with all kinds of four-legged animals on it plus reptiles and birds, he would have been repulsed by the thought of eating them.

Cornelius was a centurion of the Roman guard. As a Gentile he was considered unclean by the Jewish Law. God radically challenged Peter's beliefs by asking him to partake of unclean food and to eat in the house of an unclean Gentile.

Read Acts 10:9-23 and focus on any word that jumps out at you. Repeat that word to yourself as you begin to meditate on God's Word.

MEDITATION ♱ ENGAGE THE WORD

Meditate on Acts 10:9-10

Read the quote from Alexis Carrel. This is a great picture of prayer. But do you really feel this way about prayer? How can we change our perceptions of this sacred act? Why do you think prayer often gets the description of being boring? If your experience is different with prayer, share this with the group.

> *Prayer, like radium, is a luminous and self-generating form of energy.* —Alexis Carrel

Peter understood the true nature of prayer, because he learned the art of prayer from the Master himself. Have you had a great example of prayer in your life?

Read the quote from Frank Laubach. The story of Peter's vision displays the conversational nature of prayer. Peter spoke to God on the rooftop, and God spoke back. Besides visions, what are some other ways that God speaks to us? Have you ever had a vision?

> *Prayer at its highest is a two-way conversation—and for me the most important part is listening to God's replies.* —Frank Laubach

Meditate on Acts 10:11-16

God's request of Peter wasn't a flippant food order. God was asking Peter to break the Law of Moses, a law Peter had remained obedient to since birth, and He had good reason. What rules or laws have you religiously followed since your youth that God may be asking you to break? How do you balance tradition with new revelation from God?

Read the verse from Leviticus on page 57. This should help explain the magnitude of God's request to Peter. The dietary laws recorded by Moses and followed strictly by multiple generations of Jews were not just concerned with food, but holiness. Why would God connect holiness with food in the old covenant? How did the new covenant change this?

> I am the LORD your God; consecrate yourselves and be
> holy, because I am holy. Do not make yourselves un-
> clean by any creature that moves about on the ground.
>
> —Leviticus 11:44

Put yourself in Peter's place. How would you have reacted to God on that rooftop? Has God ever revealed something to you that changed the way you thought and acted?

Meditate on Acts 10:17-23

God didn't stop at food with Peter. He challenged his thinking again by telling him to eat with Gentiles. What group could be considered modern-day Gentiles with whom God is asking the Church to fellowship?

It is OK to tread lightly on this topic. Many voices calling for change today are laced with false motives. What are some ways you can be sure it is God, rather than your own misguided desires, changing the rules?

Read the quote from Jonathan Swift on page 58. God was showing Peter something that others weren't yet ready to see. Have you ever known something that not everyone knew yet? What did you do with that knowledge?

> *Vision is the art of seeing what is invisible to others.*
> —Jonathan Swift

How do you learn the art of true spiritual vision?

PRAYER ☦ ASK AND LISTEN

Seek the face of God. Ask, "Lord, what are You saying to us today?"

Peter received this vision from God when he was on a rooftop praying. Pray now for God's vision, His specific message for you. Then look for other times today or this week to withdraw and pray.

CONTEMPLATION ☦ REFLECT AND YIELD

What message can the Church pull from this story today? Are there things currently labeled unclean that are really clean? Why is it hard sometimes for Christians to change their perceptions on certain issues even when God reveals His truth?

GROUP STUDY

- Have you ever felt the tension between following

God's commandments and being legalistic? How do you handle this?

- Peter encountered God through prayer. What is your view of prayer, especially extended times of prayer?

- Is setting aside a time of prayer a daily practice for you? If not, why?

- Do you find that most of your prayers are one-sided? How can you turn your prayer time into a true dialogue with God?

- How are you currently responding to God as He guides and directs your life?

- Create a list of beliefs that you held about God before you were saved or early in your relationship with Him. Are there any beliefs you know are false but you can't seem to let go of them? Discuss these with a close friend or pastor.

A FAREWELL TO
FRIENDS
LISTENING FOR GOD THROUGH ACTS 20:17-38

SUMMARY

From the moment of conversion on the Damascus road,
Paul's ministry was explosive and fast-paced. He traveled the
whole stretch of the coast of the Mediterranean Sea up into
Asia Minor. He journeyed to Italy, stopping at the scattered
islands along the way, preaching the good news that the Messiah had come to both Jews and Gentiles.

Paul had spent over three years in Ephesus building the
church there and had sent word for the elders in Ephesus to
come meet him in Miletus when this passage of Acts picks up.
Paul knew hardship awaited him, but his desire to do the will
of the Father overshadowed any fear. In fact, the Spirit constantly reminded Paul that suffering was his lot, but nothing
could slow Paul down. Persecution merely fueled his passion.

The emotional farewell recorded here by Luke shows how
personally connected Paul was to the people he preached to.
He deeply cared for them and for every soul he met.

PREPARATION ⚜ FOCUS YOUR THOUGHTS

Saying good-bye is hard, especially when you don't know the
next time you will see the person. As Christians we know
that we will see each other again in heaven. How does this
thought help during times of emotional good-byes?

Does it ever feel like nothing more than wishful thinking?

READING ⚜ HEAR THE WORD

Paul sent word to the elders of Ephesus from the coastal city
of Miletus, which is located on the western shore of modern-
day Turkey where the Mediterranean and Aegean Seas meet.
Paul was waiting there for a ship to take him across the
Mediterranean so that he could get to Jerusalem.

Ephesus was a city with great history. Being founded in the
11th century B.C., it was the home to many great ancient
thinkers. It was also the home of the Temple of Artemis (Di-
ana), considered one of the wonders of the ancient world.
Christianity was brought there by Jews who had heard the
message of John the Baptist and the teaching of Apollos.
Priscilla and Aquila were well-known leaders of the church.

Paul helped solidify the church in Ephesus and spoke out
openly against the great temple, making more enemies than
friends with the local merchants who made their money from

the temple and the multitude of tourists it attracted each year. As Paul left, he commissioned Timothy to shepherd the church of Ephesus and lead them in the way of the Lord. Paul's farewell on the shores of Miletus was a farewell not just to a flock, but to friends.

Read Acts 20:17-38 quietly to yourself. Don't rush.

MEDITATION ✞ ENGAGE THE WORD

Meditate on Acts 20:17-21

Paul was directed by God to teach His word to all people, both Jews and Greeks, and Paul fulfilled this mission, although at different times he was at odds with both groups. Because he had been a zealous Pharisee, new Christians and other Gentiles feared him. Because he was an apostle of the living Christ, Jewish leaders tried to kill him.

Read the quote from Blaise Pascal. In order for people to respond to God, they need to hear His invitation. That is where you come in. How would you rate yourself in the area of sharing your faith with others?

> *Human beings must be known to be loved; but Divine beings must be loved to be known.* —Blaise Pascal

Paul reminded the leaders from Ephesus of his life example and leadership while he was with them. What would people say about you if they lived, or were friends, with you for an extended period of time? When it comes to sharing God's message, what's a good ratio for words compared to actions?

We have all probably experienced people who lived differently from what they taught. Paul was different. He did what he said, and he encouraged these new leaders to live with the same integrity. And he encourages us to do the same today.

Meditate on Acts 20:22-24

Recall the last time you were *compelled by the Spirit*. How did you know it was the Spirit prompting you? Paul often spoke of being led by the Spirit. What did he do that put him in the place to hear from God so often? What distracts you from sensing leadings from the Spirit?

Suffering was not a new part of Paul's life. From the moment of his conversion, Paul's calling included a steady dose of suffering for the name of Christ.

Read the quote from Augustine on page 65. Jesus' call also included extreme suffering. Is Christ's body, the Church, experiencing the same amount of suffering today? Now, narrow the question: Has the North American church grown complacent because of a lack of suffering? Is suffering still a part of the Church's call?

God had one Son on earth without sin, but never one
without suffering. —*Augustine*

Meditate on Acts 20:25-31

How was Paul "innocent of the blood of all men"? Paul was
adamant that he had preached the whole will of God. What
are some ways that someone could preach only a part of the
will of God?

Paul was speaking to the elders of the church in Ephesus
when he called them to be "shepherds of the church of God."
How are the pastor and other church leaders like shepherds?
In light of the priesthood of all believers, what is the difference between the minister and his or her parishioners?

Paul spoke of false prophets infiltrating the church, even from
within, upon his departure. How can we spot these wolves in
sheep's clothing? What are some ways we can distinguish
God's truth from false doctrine?

Does your church have a graceful watchdog: someone sifting
through new philosophies preserving the truth? The line between guarding the truth and holding an Inquisition is thin.
How do you maintain the truth while remaining open to new
ideas?

Meditate on Acts 20:32-38

Paul and his companions worked hard with their own hands to supply their needs and to set an example of the kind of hard work it takes to help the weak. Do you feel the Church has lost this sense of the hard work of caring for those in need? Disaster relief at home and abroad has allowed the Church to shine, but how are local churches doing at serving their own communities?

Read the quote from Henry Wadsworth Longfellow. Have you witnessed a life that was devoted to charity and gracious acts of service? Share the stories of these great examples of love with your group.

> *The life of a man consists not in seeing visions and in dreaming dreams, but in active charity and in willing service.* —Henry Wadsworth Longfellow

Paul quoted Jesus as saying, "It is more blessed to give than to receive" (v. 35). Take a moment to meditate on that phrase. Repeat the phrase softly. Do you struggle with giving versus receiving?

This passage ends with a moving scene of the elders of the church weeping and kissing Paul. Re-create this scene in your mind. Replace your picture of Paul with your own pastor or mentor. What does this scene look like in your context?

PRAYER ✝ ASK AND LISTEN

Seek the face of God. Ask, "Lord, what are You saying to us today?"

Ministers of the whole truth of God often walk through this life isolated. Pray for your pastor and other leaders of your church. Pray that they will always be faithful to the call God has placed on their lives, and praise God for the influence they have on you.

CONTEMPLATION ✝ REFLECT AND YIELD

Paul was certain of only this concerning his upcoming trip to Jerusalem: prison and hardship awaited him. Yet he did not hesitate to go. How would you react if God called you into imminent suffering? Would you go with courage and faith?

GROUP STUDY

- What would happen if your church friends and school friends got together and discussed your Christianity? Would they have the same things to say?

- Many people do not share their faith because they don't want to be pushy. What are some ways you can share your faith without being overbearing?

- Why do you think Paul had to suffer so much? What did his suffering do to his ministry?

- Have you had an experience with one of the wolves Paul was referencing? How did the distortion of truth hurt the youth group?

- Write a letter of encouragement to your pastor this week, expressing your gratitude for the hard work he or she does. Encourage others from your church to do the same.

PREACHING HIS NAME TO THE END

LISTENING FOR GOD THROUGH ACTS 28:17-31

SUMMARY

Paul had come to the last stop on his journey, Rome. In his debates and trials before Jewish and Roman officials in Jerusalem, he appealed to speak to the highest ruler in the entire world at that time. He appealed to Caesar not because he had a charge to bring against the Jews (as he explained to the Jewish leaders in Rome), but because once again he followed the leading of the Holy Spirit and put himself in the place of certain suffering for the cause of Christ.

Even house arrest did not deter Paul from preaching and setting meetings with his enemies. Paul's consistent desire for people to hear and believe the word of Jesus Christ showed the motive and compassion that drove his ministry.

Luke's recording of Paul's ministry ended there in Rome, and only legend can fill in the blanks. We can only speculate on the manner of martyrdom, but one thing we know for certain: Paul preached the name of Jesus Christ until the end.

PREPARATION ✟ FOCUS YOUR THOUGHTS

Put yourself in the shoes of first-century Jewish leaders who were listening to Paul's arguments for Jesus as the Messiah. What reservations would you have to accepting Jesus as the Anointed One? What do you think your response to Paul would have been?

READING ✟ HEAR THE WORD

Rome was the world leader during the time of Paul's missionary journeys. Caesar was a god among the people of the nations. Paul was not just an ordinary Jew held captive under Roman rule. He was a Roman citizen, entitled to the protection and benefits given to other citizens. His appeal to Caesar, made during his questioning and trial under Festus in Caesarea, placed him on the biggest stage in the world before the largest known audience. Paul made the most of this great evangelistic opportunity.

Paul also continued his writing ministry, completing his letters to the Ephesians, Philippians and Colossians, along with a personal letter to Philemon. These prison epistles shed light on Paul's experience as an "ambassador in chains" and tell stories of Paul preaching to his guards and to the Jews of Rome. Paul's work while imprisoned in Rome laid the foundation for many Christians who followed him in this capital city.

Read Acts 28:17-31. Take turns reading this passage aloud. Sense Paul's unstoppable passion for preaching the good news of Jesus Christ.

MEDITATION ✟ ENGAGE THE WORD

Meditate on Acts 28:17-22

Once he made it to Rome, though shipwrecked and under guard, Paul wasted no time in meeting with the Jews to share with them the good news of Jesus Christ. Would you have contacted the group that opposed you and was responsible for your imprisonment? What underlying passion was driving Paul through his trials?

Read the quote from Mother Teresa of Calcutta. We often want peace, but we don't want to go through the process that brings it about. Living happily with friends is not true peace. What is true peace? Why was Paul continually making contact with the enemy?

> If you want to make peace, you don't talk to your friends. You talk to your enemies.
>
> —Mother Teresa of Calcutta

Meditate on Acts 28:23-28

What lessons can you draw regarding evangelism from Paul's meetings with these Jewish leaders in Rome? What was his approach? What is the connection between Jesus and the Law of Moses? Would the gospel of the new covenant be easier to grasp if you had a greater understanding of the Old Testament?

Paul spoke of the kingdom of God. What is this Kingdom? What does it look like, and how are you a part of it today?

Read the quote from Horace Mann. Paul unswervingly followed the truth, even when it was rejected by his audience. The main source of truth for Paul was Scripture. What is your view of Scripture and truth? Does it matter what you think of the truth of the Bible?

> Keep one thing forever in view—the truth; and if you do this, though it may seem to lead you away from the opinion of men, it will assuredly conduct you to the throne of God. —Horace Mann

Read the quote from Madam Anne Soymanov Swetchine on page 73. Scripture is riddled with paradox. The Jews listening to Paul's message were left holding two apparently contradictory truths: God is one, and Jesus—whom they knew to be a man—is also God. No wonder they were divided. How can both statements be true at the same time? Do you struggle with allowing God to harmonize the paradoxes of the Bible?

> When two truths seem to directly oppose each other, we must not question either, but remember there is a third—God—who reserves to Himself the right to harmonize them.   —Madam Anne Soymanov Swetchine

Meditate on Acts 28:29-31

The last words we have from Paul paint a beautiful picture of his ministry and passion for telling the story of Jesus. What would you want the last words written about your life to say? What do you have to do now to ensure the eulogy you desire?

Read the quote from William Osler. How did Paul die daily? Have you been making the most of every day? What in your life needs to change in order for you to live with the same passion and zeal as that of the apostle Paul?

> To die daily, after the manner of St. Paul, ensures the resurrection of a new man, who makes each day the epitome of life.   —William Osler

PRAYER ☦ ASK AND LISTEN

Seek the face of God. Ask, "Lord, what are You saying to us today?"

The community you live in is full of hearts hardened to the message of Christ's love and compassion. Even those who attend church every Sunday may have hearts that are hard. Pray for the hard-hearted, that God's Spirit would soften them and that they might be open to receive the grace of God.

CONTEMPLATION ☦ REFLECT AND YIELD

Why did God's chosen people have such a hard time accepting His salvation through Jesus? Do you think we as the Church miss any messages from God because we are blinded by our own beliefs of who God is and how He should act? If yes, what do you think those messages are?

GROUP STUDY

- Is there an enemy in your life with whom you need to make peace? Is there anything holding you back from taking the first step toward peace with your enemy?

- What is your view of truth? How did you arrive at this view?

- Does your belief or disbelief in the concept of absolute truth affect your life? If yes, in what ways?

- Think of ways this week you can spread the good news of Jesus with someone else.

- If you had to sum up the main mission of the Church, what would it be? How can you fulfill this mission in your community?

- How has the message of Acts impacted your life?

Ephesians
978-0-8341-5028-7

John
978-0-8341-5022-5

Philippians
978-0-8341-5021-8

Hebrews
978-0-8341-5024-9

1 & 2 Peter
978-0-8341-5025-6

Mark
978-0-8341-5015-7

Revelation
978-0-8341-5014-0

READ IT.
STUDY IT.
LIVE IT.

Life is busy. Take a moment to slow down and listen to God. Lectio Divina, Latin for *divine reading,* is a series of Bible studies that calls students to slow down, read Scripture, meditate on it, and prayerfully respond as they listen to God through His Word. This powerful series works great in small groups and individual Bible studies!

Order *Lectio Divina for Youth* Today!